MARTIN LUTHER—
THE GREAT REFORMER

"Faith soars upward, good works are active below."

"Though not of the world, the Church lives in the world."

". . . As often as I have earnestly prayed, prayed in dead earnest, I have certainly been very freely heard and have received more than I had desired. . . . what is delayed is not denied."

"A lie is like a snowball: the longer you roll it, the larger it becomes."

"Wealth is the most insignificant thing of earth, the smallest gift that God can give a man. And yet people rush after it so madly. This is why God usually gives riches to coarse fools whom He grants nothing besides."

THE WISDOM OF

MARTIN LUTHER

PUBLISHING HOUSE
St. Louis • London

THE WISDOM OF MARTIN LUTHER

Published by Pyramid Publications
for Concordia Publishing House

Concordia edition published May, 1973

International Standard Book Number: 0-570-03166-4

Copyright © 1973 by Concordia Publishing House
All Rights Reserved

Library of Congress Catalog Card Number: 73-78850

Printed in the United States of America

Concordia Publishing House, St. Louis, Missouri 63118, U.S.A.
Concordia Publishing House, Ltd., London, E.C. 1, England

CONTENTS

GOOD NEWS FOR MAN

WHAT THE GOSPEL IS

If you ask: What is the Gospel? no better answer can be given than these words of the New Testament: Christ gave His body and shed His blood for us for the forgiveness of sins. This alone is to be preached to Christians, impressed upon them, and faithfully commended to them for constant meditation.

CHRIST AT WORK IN THE GOSPEL

Throughout the Gospel, Christ does no more than draw us out of ourselves and into Himself; He spreads His wings and invites us to take shelter under Him.

DECLARED JUST BY FAITH

WHAT IS JUSTIFICATION?

The article of justification, which is our only protection, not only against all the powers and plottings of men but also against the gates of hell, is this: by faith alone in Christ, without works, are we declared just and saved.

7

By the one solid rock which we call the doctrine of justification we mean that we are redeemed from sin, death, and the devil and are made partakers of life eternal, not by ourselves ... but by help from without, by the only-begotten Son of God, Jesus Christ.

CHRIST IS SAVIOR, NOT THE SOUL'S HANGMAN

Daily I must still work at the task of apprehending Christ. Habit does this, because for so many years I considered Him a Judge. This view has become an old, bad, rotten tree that has sunk its roots into me. Moreover, it is a teaching that accords with reason: he who commits sin should render satisfaction for it. This is natural law. . . . But in this way I lose Christ, my Savior and Comforter, and turn Him into a taskmaster and a hangman of my soul. We have now again acquired the light (of this doctrine). But when I became a doctor [of theology], I was not acquainted with it.

HOW TO BE RIGHT WITH GOD

Nothing more is required for justification than to hear of Jesus Christ and to believe on Him as our Savior.

CHRIST, CENTER OF SAVING FAITH

We were exposed [in former years] to errors of all sorts. The reason was this: we were without faith. But faith is like the center of a circle. If one strays from the center, it is impossible to keep the circle; one is bound to go wrong. The center is Christ.

WE SHALL BE ASHAMED OF OUR WEAK FAITH

On that Day [of Judgment] we shall spit upon ourselves and say: Shame on you that you were not bolder to believe Christ and to prefer all manner of evil. If I knew now the great glory that is to follow, I would let everyone walk over me.

FAITH PERTAINS TO HEAVEN, WORKS PERTAIN TO EARTH

In the way of righteousness, that is, in the kingdom of heaven, a Christian sees nothing but faith and grace. However, in the world he is thoroughly concerned about good works, diligently endeavoring to live a respectable and honest life. So faith belongs to heaven and good works belong to earth. Faith soars upward, good works are active below.

FAITH WAS THERE

In Torgau a wretched little woman once came to me and said, "Ah, dear Doctor, I have the idea that I'm lost and can't be saved because I can't believe." Then I replied, "Do you believe, dear lady, that what you pray in the Creed is true?" She answered with clasped hands, "Oh, yes, I believe it; it's most certainly true!" I replied, "Then go in God's name, dear lady. You believe more and better than I do."

FAITH IS MORE THAN KNOWLEDGE

Faith justifies not as a work, or as a quality, or as knowledge, but as assent of the will and firm confidence in the mercy of God. For if faith were only knowledge, then the devil would certainly be saved because he possesses the greatest knowledge of God and of all the works and wonders of God from the creation of the world. Accordingly faith must be understood otherwise than as knowledge. In part, however, it is assent.

FAITH IS ACTIVE IN BAPTIZED INFANTS

That works don't merit life, grace, and salvation is clear from this, that works are not spiritual birth but are fruits of this birth. We are not made sons, heirs, righteous, saints, Christians by means of works, but we do good works once we have been made, born, created such. So it's necessary to have life, salvation, and grace before works, just as a tree doesn't deserve to become a tree on account of its fruit but a tree is by nature fitted to bear fruit. Because we're born, created, generated righteous by the Word of grace, we're not fashioned, prepared, or put together as such by means of the law or works. Works merit something else than life, grace, or salvation—namely, praise, glory, favor, and certain extraordinary things— just as a tree deserves to be loved, cultivated, praised, and honored by others on account of its fruit. Urge the birth and substance of the Christian and you will at the same time extinguish the merits of works insofar as grace and salvation

from sin, death, and the devil are concerned. In-
fants who have no works are saved by faith alone,
and therefore faith alone justifies. If the power of
God can do this in one person it can do it in all,
because it's not the power of the infant but the
power of faith.

FAITH LAYS HOLD ON THE WORD

It's the devil who puts such ideas into people's
heads and says, "Ah, you must believe better. You
must believe more. Your faith is not very strong
and is insufficient." In this way he drives them to
despair. We are so constructed by nature that we
desire to have a conscious faith. We'd like to
grasp it with our hands and shove it into our
bosom, but this doesn't happen in this life. We
can't comprehend it, but we ought to apprehend
it. We should hold to the Word and let ourselves
drag along in this way.

MAN CANNOT LIVE IN A VACUUM

The heart of man is empty. Man must rely on
someone. But he cannot rely on God; therefore he
must rely on a creature.

THE ASTOUNDING NATURE OF FAITH

Our faith is an astounding thing—astounding
that I should believe Him to be the Son of God
who is suspended on the cross, whom I have never
seen, with whom I have never become acquainted.

11

Faith never fails; for when it stops in Peter [who denied that he was Jesus' disciple], it begins to rule in the robber [who was crucified with Him] (Luke 23:40).

THE PARADOX OF LAW AND GOSPEL

DIVIDING LAW AND GOSPEL

This difference between the Law and the Gospel is the height of knowledge in Christendom. Every person and all persons who assume or glory in the name of Christian should know and be able to state this difference. If this ability is lacking, one cannot tell a Christian from a heathen or a Jew; of such supreme importance is this differentiation.

LAW AND GOSPEL ARE OPPOSITES

The Law and the Gospel are two doctrines that are absolutely contrary. To place righteousness in the Law is, therefore, simply fighting against the Gospel. For the Law is an exactor, requiring of us that we should work and give; in a word, it wants to have [something] from us. But the Gospel exacts nothing of us; rather it gives freely and enjoins us to hold out our hands and to take what it offers. But now, to exact and to give, to take and to offer are opposites and cannot go on at the same time. For that which is given, I take; but that which I give, I do not take; I offer it to another. If, then, the Gospel is a gift and offers a gift, it exacts nothing. Again, the Law gives nothing but exacts of us; indeed it exacts impossible things.

WHY THE LAW SOMETIMES HAS MORE APPEAL

We are so weak that we more readily follow the feeling of sin and death than this laughter and joy of the Gospel.

To speak about myself: Redemption and the life given through Christ do not move my heart as deeply as one little word of the Law or one thought of sin and of the judgment of God terrifies my heart. The reason is that the difference between the Law and the Gospel cannot be learned well enough in practice. . . . It happens naturally that the open jaws of hell terrify us more than the open heaven elates us, that one thought of our sin causes us more sadness than almost all the sermons about the merit of Christ bring us joy.

LAW AND GOSPEL—EASY TO MIX

Oh, for the man who can distinguish well here and does not look for Law in the Gospel but keeps the two as far apart as heaven is distant from the earth! This difference is easy, certain, and plain by itself; but for us it is difficult, in fact, almost incomprehensible. To be sure, you may easily say that the Gospel is nothing but the revelation of the Son of God, the knowledge of Jesus Christ, and that it is not the revelation or the knowledge of the Law. But firmly to hold fast to this differentiation amid agony of conscience and in actual practice is a difficult task even for those who have the most experience in this matter.

EMBRACE THE PROMISES!

When in real anguish, a conscience should think of Christ and know absolutely nothing but Christ alone and should then exert its powers to the utmost to put the Law out of sight as far as it possibly can and to embrace nothing but the promise of Christ. To say this is, of course, easy; but to be able to do it in temptation, when the conscience deals with God, is the most difficult of all tasks.

CHRIST IS GOD INCARNATE

I have learned, not only through the Scriptures but also from severe inner struggles and trials, that Christ is God and has put on flesh, and likewise I have learned the doctrine of the Trinity. Today, therefore, I don't so much *believe* as I *know* through experience that these doctrines are true. In the worst temptations nothing can help us but faith that God's Son has put on flesh, is bone [of our bone], sits at the right hand of the Father, and prays for us. There is no mightier comfort. From the beginning of the world God has defended this doctrine against all heretics, who are innumerable, and defends it today against the Turk and the pope. He always confirms it by miracles, allows us to call His Son the Son of God and true

God, and hears us all when we call upon Him in Christ's name.

BIBLE READING AND HUMILITY

The Holy Scriptures require a humble reader who shows reverence and fear toward the Word of God and constantly says, "Teach me, teach me, teach me!" The Spirit resists the proud. Though they study diligently and some preach Christ purely for a time, nevertheless God excludes them from the church if they're proud. Wherefore every proud person is a heretic, if not actually, then potentially. However, it's difficult for a man who has excellent gifts not to be arrogant. Those whom God adorns with great gifts He plunges into the most severe trials in order that they may learn that they're nothing. . . . Pride drove the angels out of heaven and spoils many preachers. Accordingly it's humility that's needed in the study of sacred literature.

BIBLE INTERPRETATION

No violence should be done the words of God, neither by a man nor by an angel; but as far as possible we should retain them in their simplest meaning and take them in their grammatical and literal sense, unless an obvious circumstance plainly forbids it, lest we give our adversaries occasion to make a mockery of all Scripture.

If no adoration is involved, images may be used just as writings which put us in mind of facts and, as it were, picture them to us. The Gospels place the story of Christ before us, and the Law and the Prophets place the will of God before us. But who for this reason kisses the paper? Who adores it? Who imagines that he is rendering God a service if he falls down before the Holy Bible? Different is its use. It is to be read that we may learn to know the will of God and do it.

THE WORD, ONLY AUTHORITY

I shall and must be convinced by Scripture, not by the unreliable life and teachings of men, no matter how holy they may be.

SIN: CAUSE, CONSEQUENCE, CURE

SIN CORRUPTS THE WHOLE MAN

Holy Scripture declares that sin came from the devil, whom, contrary to God's Word, our parents obeyed. They became disobedient to God and thereby brought terrible punishment upon themselves. For through this sin [of the Fall] not only our bodies have become so weakened that they have changed from immortal into mortal bodies, but the intellect, heart, mind, and will are entirely corrupted and turned evil. For man has lost the right and true knowledge of God. Moreover, his will is so entirely corrupted that he desires and wants nothing but that which is evil.

THE REASON WE MUST DIE

If Eve had not sinned, we would nonetheless have eaten, drunk, slept, etc., but all this without any sin and disorder. Such a life would have continued as long as it pleased God, let us say for two or three thousand years. Then we would have been changed in a moment without passing through death; and, completely sanctified, we would have entered into an eternal life free from trouble, such a life as, indeed, we are even now expecting. But because sin has stolen into the world through the work of the devil and the consent of man, the judgment has been passed from the beginning and remains in force throughout this life: "In the day that thou eatest thereof thou shalt surely die" (Gen. 2:17). This is the reason why we must die.

PLAYING GOD: MAN'S CHIEF SIN

No sin troubles us as severely as the lust after divinity. Of course, the lust of the flesh is also a furiously strong urge, yet it is only a form [of sin] and nothing in comparison with spiritual lust or fornication.

WHAT NO ONE NEEDS TO LEARN

Nothing is easier than sinning.

After baptism original sin is like a wound which has begun to heal. It is really a wound, yet it is becoming better and is constantly in the process of healing, although it is still festering, is painful, etc. So original sin remains in the baptized until their death, although it is in the process of being rooted out. It is rendered harmless, and so it cannot accuse or damn us.

THE UNFORGIVABLE SIN

The sin which Judas committed when he betrayed Christ was a small sin because it could be forgiven. But to despair of grace is a greater sin because it cannot be forgiven, for God has determined for Christ's sake to forgive the sin of those who believe. This sin is so great and wicked that it leads either to despair or to presumption. Consequently one ought to be disposed to say, "It is true. I have sinned. But I will not despair on this account or commit the sin again." However, it's a calumny to conclude from these words of mine that it is permissible to sin and then to believe, for one can't believe in Christ unless one declares and resolves not to sin again. Sin carries us down to despair or up to presumption. In either case the sin is not repented of, for sin is either exaggerated or not acknowledged by all.

NEVER DESPAIR BECAUSE OF SIN?

We should not become despondent or despair because of our sin and because we are great sinners; for God has caused the forgiveness of sins to be publicly proclaimed to all who honestly recognize and confess their sins and to be offered to everybody, no one excluded. Nor will He change His mind. He remains true in His Word forever and ever and keeps faith with men.

JESUS CHRIST: SON OF GOD, SAVIOR

LOOK FOR GOD IN CHRIST!

One should think of no other God than Christ. The god who does not speak through Christ is not God. In Old Testament times God would hear prayers because of the mercy seat (Exodus 25); just so He will hear no one except through Christ. But the greater part of the Jews ran hither and thither, burned incense and offered sacrifices here and there in order to serve God. They looked for God in many places, to the neglect of the mercy seat. So it is now. Men search for God everywhere; but because they do not search for Him in Christ, they do not find Him.

WHO CAN SAY HOW MUCH HE SUFFERED?

Oh, the disciples did not have exceptional cares. They had sympathy with Christ when they noticed how He acted. But sleep overpowered them. They were as some who watch at a sickbed. They express their sympathy, but they often fall asleep while the sick person cannot sleep. Therefore He comes three times and asks them to stay awake: Please do not sleep! Why do you not talk to Me? Ah, it is a great weakness in Christ to call upon those for help whom He has created! The heart of no man can entirely comprehend what sort of suffering it was that it brought on a bloody sweat. Those were our sins which He bore.

HE STEPPED INTO OUR PLACE

Because Christ was born a man for our sake and was sent by God to help us from sin and death, He had to step into our place and become a Sacrifice for us, and He Himself had to bear, and render satisfaction for, the wrath and the curse into which we had fallen and under which we lay.

ALL DEPENDS ON THE RESURRECTION

He who would preach the Gospel must go directly to preaching the resurrection of Christ. He who does not preach the resurrection is no apostle, for this is the chief part of our faith. . . . The greatest importance attaches to this article of faith. For were there no resurrection, we would have neither comfort nor hope, and everything else Christ did and suffered would be in vain.

CHRIST'S PROPER KINGDOM

Christ is not concerned with political and domestic economy but is a king who is to destroy the dominion of the devil and is to save men. But He feigns to be rather much of a simpleton at doing it.

IT'S EASY TO MISTAKE HIS RULE

The Man who sits at the right hand of the Father (Ps. 110:1) insists on ruling, but the world will not put up with Him and says: "We will not have this man to reign over us" (Luke 19:4). Yet He must rule for the sake of Him who says: "Sit Thou at My right hand" (Ps. 110:1). Moreover, this King acts as if He were down and were being ruled over by everybody, as if He were completely impotent. And yet that which has been written stands: "Whatsoever the Lord pleased, that did He in heaven and in earth" (Ps. 135:6). Who is wise? He who understands this rule.

CONCEPT OF THE CHURCH

WHO IS THE CHURCH?

God's people and the church are those who rely on nothing else than God's grace and mercy.

CHRISTIANS—PERFECT YET IMPERFECT

The church is holy and is called holy according to its first fruits, not according to its tithes and fullness. It is holy by faith in the name of Christ, in whom it enjoys purity. In itself it does not have purity, but it is holy for the sake of His name. For sins are latent in the saints—sins, however, that have been subjected and do not rule, though sins which, it is true, at times break out by moving Christians to impatience, sadness, despair, etc.

GOOD-BYE, CHURCH PERFECTIONISTS!

Farewell to those who want an entirely pure and purified church. This is plainly wanting no church at all.

KNOWN BY FAITH—NOT BY SIGHT

The existence of the church is an article of faith; for it is apprehended by faith, not by sight. Besides, God hides the church in astounding ways, now by sins, now by dissensions and errors, now by infirmity, offenses, deaths of the pious, and the great number of the impious, etc.

NOT OF BUT IN THE WORLD

God has placed His church into the midst of the world, among an infinite variety of activities and vocations, so that Christians might not turn into monks but might live in ordinary society and our works and the practices of faith might become known among men.

HOW TO HAVE A TRUE CHURCH

Let him who wants a true church cling to the Word by which everything is upheld.

GOD'S MEN IN THE GOSPEL MINISTRY

GOD'S POWER IN FRAIL MEN

Our Lord God fills His high office in an odd manner. He entrusts it to preachers, poor sinners, who tell and teach the message and yet live according to it only in weakness. Thus God's power always goes forward amid extreme weakness.

THE BURDENS OF A MINISTER

If I wanted to write about the burdens of a minister as I know and have experienced them, I would frighten all away from the office. For a good minister must hazard everything, so that nothing is dearer to him than Christ and eternal life and that, after he has lost this life and everything, Christ may say: "Come to Me, son." I hope He will speak this way to me, too, on that Day, for here [in this life] He speaks very unkindly to me. I am burdened with the entire world, with the emperor and the pope.

THE BIBLE, A BOOK OF BLESSINGS

TWO CARDINAL CONCEPTS IN THE BIBLE

The entire Bible has two principal thoughts. The first: Human nature is in its entirety damned and ruined by sin, nor can it come out of this calamity and death by its own powers and efforts. The second: God alone is just and out of mercy destroys sin and justifies.

HOW ALL THINGS BEGAN

A strong argument for faith in Scripture is this: that only Scripture tells how life goes on and of what a thing consists. No Demosthenes or Cicero tells how the world, man, woman, were created and how all things are constituted and go on.

RICH IN CONTENT

The Bible is the proper book for men. There the truth is distinguished from error far more clearly than anywhere else, and one finds something new in it every day. For twenty-eight years, since I became a doctor [of theology], I have now constantly read and preached the Bible; and yet I have not exhausted it but find something new in it every day.

LIKE BRANCHES FULL OF FRUIT

For a number of years I have now annually read through the Bible twice. If the Bible were a large, mighty tree and all its words were little branches, I have tapped at all the branches, eager to know what was there and what it had to offer.

THE BIBLE IN A CLASS BY ITSELF

Holy Scripture is full of divine gifts and virtues. All the books of the Gentiles teach nothing whatever about faith, hope, and charity. In fact, they know nothing about these divine virtues. They look only at that which lies before them. "Trust, hope in the Lord" (Ps. 42:5)! Even if we had only the Psalter and Job, we would certainly see my point. . . . In short, Holy Scripture is the greatest and the divine book, full of consolations for all trials; for about faith it teaches differently from what reason can see, about hope differently from what reason can think, about love differently from what reason can expect. More than this. It teaches these virtues to shine forth in days of adversity, for it points to the existence of another life beyond this miserable one.

PRAYER—KEY TO BIBLE READING

That the Holy Scriptures cannot be penetrated by study and talent is most certain. Therefore your first duty is to begin to pray, and to pray to this effect that if it please God to accomplish something for His glory—not for yours or any other person's—He very graciously grant you a true understanding of His words. For no master of the divine words exists except the Author of these words, as He says: "They shall be all taught by God" (John 6:45 RSV). You must, therefore, completely despair of your own industry and ability and rely solely on the inspiration of the Spirit.

EXPERIENCE HELPS OUR UNDERSTANDING

No one understands Scripture unless it is brought home to him, that is, unless he experiences it.

PRAYER PROMISES

LITTLE SIGH—MIGHTY PRAYER

A Christian is always praying whether he is sleeping or waking; for his heart is always praying, and even a little sigh is a great and mighty prayer. For so God says: "For the sighing of the needy now will I arise, saith the Lord." (Ps. 12:5)

WHAT PRAYER ACCOMPLISHES

Whatever good may be done is done and brought about by prayer, which alone is the omnipotent empress. In human affairs we accomplish everything through prayer. What has been properly arranged we keep in order, what has gone amiss we change and improve, what cannot be changed and improved we bear, overcoming all

the trouble and sustaining all the good by prayer.
Against force there is no help but prayer alone.

DELAY IS NOT DENIAL

No one believes how great the power and the
efficacy of our prayer are unless he has learned it
by experience. It is a great thing when a man who
feels himself in dire need can turn to prayer. This
I know: As often as I have earnestly prayed,
prayed in dead earnest, I have certainly been very
freely heard and have received more than I had
desired. To be sure, at times our Lord God has delayed a little while; yet He has heard. What is delayed is not denied.

RECEIVING SOMETHING BETTER

All who pray to God in faith are heard and receive that for which they have asked, although
not in the hour or at the time or in the manner or
in the matter which they desire. Yet they receive
something better and more glorious than they
dared hope for. Paul testifies to this: "We know
not what we should pray for as we ought" (Rom.
8:26) because we do not know by what or in
which way we would be better served. . . . Therefore God certainly hears those who pray in faith,
yet not in the hour, the manner, and the matter
which they prescribe to Him but when and how it
appears to Him to be good for us. Then, too, we
may be certain of this: If what we ask for will hal-
low His name and glorify His kingdom and is according to His will, He assuredly hears us. But if

we ask for anything contrary to this, we are not heard; for God does nothing contrary to His name, kingdom, and will.

THE MIRACLE OF LOVE

HOW GREAT GOD'S LOVE!

Our Lord God must be a pious Man to be able to love rascals. I cannot do it, and yet I am a rascal myself.

CHRISTIANS LOVE EVEN THEIR ENEMIES

To love him who loves us is the law of nature; to love enemies sincerely is characteristic of the children of God. To love God is to love our closest Friend.

WHEN LOVE SPEAKS UP

Christian love cannot hold its tongue nor bear to see its neighbor err and sin. It must rebuke and improve wherever it can.

LOVE OVERLOOKS FAULTS

Affection for our fellowman is to be like the chaste love with which one spouse loves the other. In this relation all faults are rationalized and covered, and only the virtues are seen.

GOOD WORKS AS FRUITS
OF FAITH

GOOD WORKS DEFINED

Good works are works that flow from faith and from the joy of heart that has come to us because we have forgiveness of sins through Christ.

WHAT GOD PRESCRIBES IS A GOOD WORK

Everybody should consider precious and glorious whatever God commands, even though it were no more than picking a wisp of straw from the ground.

FAITH MAKES THE DIFFERENCE

Faith exists before works and is necessary for their performance. But works may often be done without faith. For in Matt. 24:24 Christ predicted that men would come who would do signs and wonders in order to lead even the elect into error, if that were possible. Therefore we must not rely on any works or miracles unless they are produced by faith and further faith.

GOOD INTENTIONS NOT ENOUGH

Good intentions are of no value; one must first have God's Word and be certain that what one does is good to do.

GOOD WORKS IN EVERYDAY LIFE

If, then, there are passages in Holy Scripture which seem to teach that we must render satisfaction through works, apply such passages to worldly relations in the home or in temporal government, commend them to fathers and mothers; but do not make such works be a payment for your sin before God. Here there is no bearing and paying; the Lamb bears everything.

THE WORTH OF WORKS DONE IN FAITH

When the matter about consideration is not justification, we cannot praise highly enough the good works God prescribed. For who can sufficiently praise the usefulness and the fruit of only one deed a Christian does out of faith and in faith? It is more precious than heaven and earth. . . . But the works that are done outside faith, though in appearance they seem to be very holy, are under sin and the curse of God. Therefore the people who perform them—far from meriting grace, righteousness, and life eternal by them—are rather heaping sin upon sin.

COUNSEL ON MARRIAGE
AND FAMILY LIFE

HOW LUTHER PRIZED HIS WIFE

I would not want to exchange my Kate for France nor for Venice to boot; to begin with (1) because God has given her to me and me to her; (2) because I often find out that there are more shortcomings in other women than in my Kate; and although she, of course, has some too, these are nonetheless offset by far greater virtues; (3) because she keeps faith and honor in our marriage relation.

CLOSING AN EYE HERE AND THERE

In domestic and political economy the rule must be that one does not want anything done that is wrong. But if it is done, it must be met with the forgiveness of sins; otherwise one spoils things. A married man must close his eyes to many things in his wife and children, and yet order must not be neglected. This principle obtains in all walks of life. The forgiveness of sins is in all creatures. Not all trees grow straight; not all waters flow straight; nor is the earth level everywhere. Therefore, the statement is true, "He who does not know how to close an eye does not know how to rule." This is gentleness. One must put up with much and yet not pass over everything. It is said, "Neither everything nor nothing."

TROUBLE IN AND OUT OF MARRIAGE

He who takes a wife is not entering a life of ease but is creating trouble for himself. It is true, the continence of celibacy is not the smallest temptation a man is called on to endure, as those know who have experienced it. On the other hand, the molestations of married life are intolerable to men. Therefore Socrates is reported to have wisely replied to him who was going about looking for a wife: Whether you marry or not, you will repent of what you have done. In Paradise marriage would have been most delightful. The heat and fury of sexual desire would not have been so intense there; flesh and blood would have been different. But we are so contaminated by original sin that there is not a walk of life which at times does not cause the person who has entered it to feel regretful. Our original sin, which has defiled and ruined our entire human nature, is to blame for this. It seems to me that the most delightful walk of life is to be found in a household of moderate means, to live there with an obliging wife and to be satisfied with little. . . . Alas, dear God, how will You properly arrange conditions to please us?

It is the highest grace of God when lo ues to flourish in married life. The first dent, is an intoxicating love, so that we ed and drawn to marriage. After we have slept off our intoxication, sincere love remains in the married life of the godly; but the godless are sorry they ever married.

THRIFT, THE BEST INCOME

The husband should earn, but the wife should save. That is why a wife may indeed make her husband rich, but not the husband the wife; for a penny saved is better than a penny earned. Thus thrift is the best income.

TRIBUTE TO WOMANHOOD

WOMAN'S GREATEST HONOR

Through the Holy Spirit Adam called his wife by the excellent name of Eve, that is, mother. He does not say woman, but mother, and adds "of all the living" (Gen. 3:20). Here you have the true distinction of womanhood, to wit, to be the source of all living human beings. The words are brief, yet they are an oration such as neither Demosthenes nor Cicero ever composed. But this oration is by the Holy Spirit, who is most eloquent; and yet it is worthy of our first parent. The Holy Spirit is to deliver the address at this point. If *this* Orator

ARDENT LOVE OFTEN COOLS QUICKLY

It is the highest grace of God when love continues to flourish in married life. The first love is ardent, is an intoxicating love, so that we are blinded and drawn to marriage. After we have slept off our intoxication, sincere love remains in the married life of the godly; but the godless are sorry they ever married.

THRIFT, THE BEST INCOME

The husband should earn, but the wife should save. That is why a wife may indeed make her husband rich, but not the husband the wife; for a penny saved is better than a penny earned. Thus thrift is the best income.

TRIBUTE TO WOMANHOOD

WOMAN'S GREATEST HONOR

Through the Holy Spirit Adam called his wife by the excellent name of Eve, that is, mother. He does not say woman, but mother, and adds "of all the living" (Gen. 3:20). Here you have the true distinction of womanhood, to wit, to be the source of all living human beings. The words are brief, yet they are an oration such as neither Demosthenes nor Cicero ever composed. But this oration is by the Holy Spirit, who is most eloquent; and yet it is worthy of our first parent. The Holy Spirit is to deliver the address at this point. If *this* Orator so defines and praises woman, we may in fairness cover up whatever frailties she has.

HUSBANDS SHOULD NOT ABDICATE

My wife can persuade me to do whatever she pleases, for she has the entire household in her hand. And indeed I gladly grant her the complete control of domestic affairs, but despite this I intend to preserve my right intact. The rule of women has never done any good.

God made Adam the lord of all creatures; but when Eve persuaded him to become lord also over God, she spoiled everything. For this we must thank you women who lure men on by cunning and tricks.

SINGING THE PRAISE OF WOMAN

The Holy Spirit praises woman, as, for example, Judith, Esther, Sarah. And among the heathen Lucretia and Artemisia were praised. Without women marriage would be impossible. Taking a wife is a remedy for fornication. A woman is a pleasant life companion. Women bear children and are wont to educate them and to administer domestic affairs. Moreover, they are inclined to be merciful; for they were appointed by God to bear children, to please man, and to be compassionate.

WOMEN OFTEN THE MORE ZEALOUS CHRISTIANS

When the female sex begins to embrace Christian doctrine, it is more fervent in faith than the who by their ruthless practices have checked many highly gifted pupils.

GOD GIVES PARENTS A PATTERN

A father should handle his children in the manner in which we observe God handling us. God at times afflicts and chastises us, but He does not kill us; and in the midst of the affliction He consoles, strengthens, confirms, nourishes, and favors us. And when we have committed any sin against Him, He does not punish us according to the rigor of the Law but tempers the punishments. Moreover, when we have repented, He instantly remits the sins as well as the punishments. In the same manner parents ought to handle their children.

CHILDREN HAVE UNQUESTIONING FAITH

In all simplicity and without any disputing, children believe that God is gracious and that there is an eternal life. Oh, what a blessing comes to the children who die at this time! Such a death would, of course, cause me extreme sorrow, because a part of my body and the mother's body would die. These natural affections do not cease in the pious, as those who are without feeling and are hardened imagine, for such affections are the work of divine creation. Children live with all sincerity in faith, without the interference of reason, as Ambrose [Bishop of Milan, +397 A.D.] says: There is a lack of reason but not of faith.

DISCIPLINE IN SCHOOL

Some teachers are as cruel as hangmen. I was once beaten fifteen times before noon, without any fault of mine, because I was expected to decline and conjugate [Latin verbs] although I had not yet been taught this. Anthony Tucher of Nürnberg was accustomed to say, "Praise and punishment belong together; one should be very friendly to people and yet at the same time be ready to whip them."

CHILDREN WHO WON'T LEARN

Solomon said, "Discipline your son while there is hope; do not set your heart on his destruction" (Prov. 19:18). As long as there is hope, one should push a child forward. But if one sees that there's no hope, that the child can't learn, one shouldn't flog him to death on that account but should accustom him to something else.

GOVERNMENT UNDER GOD

HONORING THE STATE

These three—the ministry of the Word, the state, and marriage—God wanted to set in order again before Judgment Day. For since the times of the apostles the office of the state has never been praised in the manner in which we have praised it.

THE SECRET OF A SUCCESSFUL GOVERNMENT

A government is controlled either by a few or by many; and yet if God does not control it, it is not administered well either by a few or by many.

PRAYER A BETTER DEFENSE THAN GUNS

I do not place my hope on our guns and ramparts, but on the Lord's Prayer. It must defeat the enemy; the Ten Commandments will not do so. I hope that when the time will have come for our Lord God to hear our prayer, the enemy will have to fall because of internal dissension. . . . For in this way all empires in the world have fallen. . . . None went down by force; dissension and division did the damage.

GOD USES KINGS AS PAWNS

God looks upon kings as children look upon playing cards. While they are playing, they hold the cards in their hands; thereafter they fling them into a corner, under the bench, or into the rubbish. God also acts in this way with potentates. While they rule, He considers them good; but as soon as they overdo it, He "puts down the mighty from their seats" (Luke 1:52) and lets them lie there as discards.

LYING BY LIPS AND LIFE

LIKE A SNOWBALL

A lie is like a snowball: the longer you roll it, the larger it becomes.

MAN LIVES IN A WORLD OF LIES

Man is a liar actively and passively, that is, he tells a lie and he suffers a lie; for he who relies on the children of men is deceived.

LYING CALLS FOR A GOOD MEMORY

A liar must have a good memory, because everyone is justified or condemned by his words.

DEFAMATION

Picture the scene to yourself. When defamers come together, their entertainment consists in taking someone, placing him in their midst, and taking turns at tearing him apart with their teeth, as dogs tear the cadaver of a horse in the field. . . . For shame, for shame! What a horrid monster a defamer is!

EXCUSES FOR TALEBEARING

When people slander others, they remark: I do not say this because I wish to slander him, nor do I want to have it told behind his back. Fine talkers these, who with a rhetorical coloring deny

that they are saying what they are saying very
emphatically, and denying that they are saying it
in the very manner in which they are saying it. . . .
Others commend their action by saying that what
they are relating is, after all, the truth. . . . But
why do you not publicly confess your own sins,
since these too are true? Do you love your neighbor as yourself? About his defects (because of the
truth) you hold you should not be silent, but
about yours you hold you should be. Behold how
beautifully you are condemning yourself!

HOW TO TREAT GOSSIP

In the Bible we are taught the best of comfort
when we are oppressed by slander. We are taught
to commit our cause to God and not to be sad or
worried or storm about it. It is sufficient to know
that we are carrying on the cause of God. Let us
then divide the suffering with these slanderers in
this way that we are vexed by them without while
they are vexed by themselves within.

THE BENEFIT OF THE DOUBT

We should not, as detractors habitually do, ex-
aggerate the evil men do; we should extenuate it
as much as possible in order to show that we are
sorry about the misery of the perpetrators rather
than personally indignant. For the Holy Spirit is
kind. He does not glory in the evil others do; He
glories in His kindness. He has mercy on all.

WORRIES, TROUBLESOME THOUGHTS

THEY GRIND ONE DOWN

Albert, Archbishop of Mayence, used to say that the human heart is like a millstone. If you pour grain on the stone, it revolves, crushes and powders it, and turns it into flour. But if no grain is there, the stone revolves anyway; but now it crushes itself and becomes thinner, smaller, and narrower. In like manner, the human heart wants something to do. If it does not have the works of its calling to perform, the devil comes and shoots temptation, melancholy, and sadness into it. And then the heart consumes itself with sadness. It pines away, and many a man worries himself to death.

COMBATING WORRIES

When I'm troubled by thoughts which pertain to political questions or household affairs, I take up a psalm or a text of Paul and fall asleep over it. But the thoughts which come from Satan demand more of me. Then I have to resort to more difficult maneuvers before I extricate myself, although I easily get the upper hand in thoughts of an economic or domestic character.

There are two kinds of blasphemy. First, there is active blasphemy when we consciously and intentionally look for reasons to blaspheme. . . . God keep us from this! But, second, blasphemy is passive when the devil introduces such perverse thoughts into our heads against our will and in spite of our struggle against them. By means of these thoughts God wishes to occupy us so that we don't get lazy and snore but fight against them and pray. But when the end of life approaches, these temptations cease, for then the Holy Spirit is near to His Christians, keeps the devil at a distance, and gives us a tranquil and quiet mind. . . . Consequently, even if we are not perfectly holy, Christ will wash away our sins with His blood and, when we depart from this life, will make us altogether pure in the life to come. In the meantime we are content with the righteousness which exists in hope through faith in Jesus Christ.

THOUGHTS IN SICKNESS

We who believe in Him should by all means be confident, for we know that we do not belong to ourselves but to Him who died for us. Therefore if we are sick, we are not sick unto ourselves; if we are well, we are not well unto ourselves; if we are in troubles, we are not in troubles unto ourselves; if we are glad, we are not glad unto ourselves. In a word, whatever happens to us does not happen to us but to Him who died for us and has made us His own. In like manner, when a pious child is sick or suffers from some trouble, it is sicker to the parents than to itself; its trouble strikes the parents harder than the child, because the child is not its own but belongs to the parents. . . . He on whom we believe is almighty.

CHRISTIAN CHEERFULNESS

A Christian should and must be a cheerful person. If he isn't, the devil is tempting him. I have sometimes been grievously tempted while bathing in my garden, and then I have sung the hymn, "Let us now praise Christ." Otherwise I would have been lost then and there. Accordingly, when you notice that you have some such thoughts, say, "This isn't Christ." To be sure, he can hear the name of Christ, but it's a lie because Christ says, "Let not your hearts be troubled" [John 14:27]; "Trust in me," etc. This is a command of God: "Rejoice!" I now preach this, and I also write it, but I haven't as yet learned it. But it happens that we learn as we're tempted. If we were always glad, the devil would befoul us. Christ knows that our hearts are troubled, and it is for this reason that he says and commands, "Let not your hearts be troubled."

Thus we are like the holy fathers in our faith. The weaker we are than the fathers, the greater the victory Christ obtains for us. We are very inexperienced, very weak, and very proud over against the devil; he has a great advantage over us, for our wisdom, power, and holiness are not so great as our fathers' were. But our Lord God wants to put an end to the devil's extreme arrogance. Paul had to say, "I alone have resisted all the derision of Satan."

GOOD FROM EVIL

IN MARRIAGE

See whether this is true: God uses all evil for good, but man and the devil use all good for evil. God drives man to marriage by means of sensual desire. Otherwise, if it were not for love, who would get married? Afterward man's appetite is curbed somewhat so that he doesn't commit adultery with other women.

IN POLITICS

God snatches man by means of ambition to become a magistrate. Otherwise who would seek this office? After a while his ambition is kept within the bounds of his authority, he doesn't seek what belongs to others, and he doesn't injure his own people, but there must be an inclination and a desire there.

IN ONE'S OCCUPATION

God compels man to seek a better living by means of greed. Otherwise who would do anything if he wished for nothing or could keep none of his possessions? In a little while man's greed, too, is kept within limits.

God drives man to faith by means of fear and despair. Except for pride and envy, which are simply devilish, God uses these evils for good by antiperistasis, that is, He does not use the subjects in whom these qualities exist but He uses the objects that are persecuted by them. For so God troubles the saints through the devil and his followers. On the other hand, the devil uses God Himself and all good things for evil: chastity and celibacy for hypocrisy, humility for pride, love for sects and sedition, poverty for luxury and idleness.

THE PSEUDOSCIENCE OF ASTROLOGY

OBJECTIONS TO ASTROLOGY

There are many reasons I can't believe astrologers, and of these the principal reasons are the following: *First,* the calendars never agree. One astrologer prophesies that it will be warm, another that it will be cold. I think it should be understood that this is so: it's cold outside and warm behind the stove. *Second,* when a child is born, the rays of all the signs above the horizon or of all the planets or stars are said to reach that child. For the child is, as it were, a poppy seed in comparison with the smallest star. Now, I ask, why is it that all stars don't affect that child equally if all reach him equally? *Third,* why does the effect occur outside of the uterus, at the very hour and minute when the infant comes out of the uterus, and not in the uterus? Shouldn't the stars have influence in the uterus as well as outside of it? Do you mean to suggest that the stars care about a little skin on the woman's belly when otherwise the sun gives life to every member? *Fourth*, Esau and Jacob were born under one sign and in rapid succession. Where did the diversity of their natures come from? The astrologers rack their brains about this but they can't offer a solid explanation.

ASTROLOGY, NOT A SCIENCE

I could never be persuaded to count astrology among the sciences, for it has no clear proof. The fact that men adduce experience does not impress me, for all astrological experiences are merely particular instances. Those skilled in this field have noted and put into writing the predictions that have not failed; the other experiences, in which they were wrong, which were not followed by the results they had predicted would certainly come, they did not note. But just as Aristotle says that one swallow does not make a summer, so I do not think one can make a science out of such isolated observations. It is said of hunters that they may go hunting every day but do not find game every day. Obviously, the same thing may be said of astrologers and their predictions; for they fail very often.

46

FALSE TRUST

To believe the stars is idolatry, for it is against the First Commandment: "Thou shalt have no other gods before Me."

SUPERSTITION

Since the devil is always aping God and trying to imitate and improve everything God does, he too took outward things that were to be means of holiness. . . . Bells are to drive away the devils in storms; St. Anthony's knives stab the devil; the blessing of herbs drives away poisonous worms; certain blessings heal cows, ward off milk thieves, put out fires; certain writings give security in war and, at other times, against iron, fire, water, wild beasts, etc. . . . People believe more easily and more gladly in his [devil's] promises, in his sacraments, in his prophets, than in Christ's. He is the great god of the world. Christ calls him "prince of the world" (John 12:31), and Paul speaks of him as "god of this world." (2 Cor. 4:4)

DREAMS AND SIGNS

This is where dreams come from: Man's spirit can't rest, for Satan is there even when man is asleep, though angels are also present. The devil can so frighten me that sweat pours from me in my sleep. I don't pay attention to either dreams or signs. I have the Word, and that I let suffice. I don't want an angel to come to me. I wouldn't believe him now anyway, although the time may come when I would desire it in special circumstances. I don't say that dreams and signs are of value at other times, nor do I care, for we already have everything we should have in the Scriptures. Troubled dreams are of the devil, because everything that serves death and terror and murder and lies is the devil's handiwork.

Satan has often distracted me from prayer and has put such thoughts into my head that I ran away from it. The most severe bouts I have had with him I had when I was in bed at my Katy's side.

ABOUT FEARING FUTURE EVENTS

Even if astrologers offered something certain, what folly it is to be so anxious about the future! For even granting that it is possible to know the future through astrological predictions, would it not in many ways be far better, if they are evil, to be completely ignorant of them than to know them, as Cicero, too, contends? It is better always to live in the fear of God and to pray than to be tormented by the fear of future events.

CARE AND CURE OF HUMAN LIFE

EVERY SEVENTH YEAR LIFE CHANGES

My Hans is about to enter upon his seventh year, which is always climacteric, that is, a time of change. People always change every seventh year. The first period of seven years is childhood, and at

the second change—say, in the fourteenth year—
boys begin to look out into the world; this is the
time of boyhood, when the foundations are laid in
the arts. At the age of twenty-one youths desire
marriage, in the twenty-eighth year young men
are householders and heads of families, while at
the age of thirty-five men have civil and ecclesias-
tical positions. This continues to the age of forty-
two, when we are kings. Soon after this men begin
to lose their sense. So every seventh year always
brings to man some new condition and way of life.
This has happened to me, and it happens to
everybody.

EVERY AGE OF MAN HAS ITS PET SINS

Young fellows are tempted by girls, men who
are thirty years old are tempted by gold, those of
forty by honor and glory, and those who are sixty
think: If only I were pious now!

HUMAN LIFE IS FULL OF MISERY

Great is the misery of human life. Nothing were
better than a blessed death to pass away and let
the world have its heartache. . . . In short, human
life is madness. When children, we were troubled
by childish complaints; when young men, we
were dying of love; when old men, we became
worse, that is, we turn into misers and worshipers
of mammon.

THE DUTY OF PRESERVING HEALTH

A man's life and the health of his organs and the proper condition of his body are gifts of God, the Creator. Therefore care is to be taken particularly of one's health. In Col. 2:23 Paul disputes with the hypocrites, who did not give the body its due, and with the Epicureans, who killed it by luxurious living.

THE VALUE OF EXERCISE

Moving about produces health; and health makes one move about.

THE USE AND MISUSE OF MONEY

WHAT WE HAVE IS REALLY GOD'S

If a man has the goods of this world, he may say before men: This is mine. But before God it is necessary to say: God, this is Thine.

MONEY, THE DEVIL'S MAGIC WORD

Money is the word through which the devil created everything in this world, just as God creates things through the true Word.

PEOPLE ARE MONEY-MAD

Everybody is concerned about piling up much money for himself. Produce and victuals these avaricious folk do not value so highly as money, although they cannot devour it. And yet the world considers money of sole importance, as though body and soul depended on it. God and one's neighbor are despised, and mammon is served.

WEALTH, ONE OF GOD'S LESSER GIFTS

Wealth is the most insignificant thing on earth, the smallest gift that God can give a man. What is it in comparison with the Word of God? Indeed, what is it in comparison even with gifts of the body, such as beauty? What is it in comparison with gifts of the soul? And yet people rush after it so madly. It is the material, formal, efficient, and final motive of men; and yet there is nothing good in it. This is why God usually gives riches to coarse fools whom He grants nothing besides.

WIDESPREAD STEALING

Stealing is the commonest way of making a living in this world.

THE DECEIVING GLAMOR OF WEALTH

A man who has devoted himself to the wealth and honor of the world, meanwhile forgetting his soul and his God, resembles a little child which holds in its hand a beautifully shaped and colored apple and fancies it has something good. But on the inside the apple is rotten and full of worms.

WHO IS A RICH MAN?

No one is rich be he emperor or pope, except the man who is rich in God.

WORK, LEISURE, SENSE OF VOCATION

GOD PROVIDES—THROUGH MAN'S WORK

To put it briefly, God wants people to work. If you did not farm or work, you would have to lie behind the stove a long time in order to have anything given to you. It is true, of course, that God could support you without work, could let fried and boiled foods, corn, and wine grow on the table for you. But He will not do this. He wants you to work and to use your reason in this matter. This also applies to preaching and to all other things. He gives us wool, letting it grow for us on the sheep. But the wool is not immediately converted into cloth. We must work it up to make cloth of it. When the cloth is there, it does not promptly become a coat. First the tailor must make it. And so on; in everything God acts in such a way that He will provide, but we should work.

NO PREJUDICE AGAINST PROPERTY

It is right to work in order to acquire possessions.

GOD WANTS NO IDLENESS

We must note well the words of the Lord. He does say: Do not worry! But He does not say: Do not work! Worry is forbidden, but not work. In fact, we are commanded and enjoined so to work that the perspiration flows over our nose. God does not want man to be idle.

IN DEFENSE OF REST AND LEISURE

We also serve God by doing nothing, in fact, in no way more than by doing nothing. For this reason He, above all things, wanted the Sabbath so rigidly kept.

MEANING OF CHRISTIAN VOCATION

To serve God simply means to do what God has commanded and not to do what God has forbidden. And if only we would accustom ourselves properly to this view, the entire world would be full of service to God, not only the churches but also the home, the kitchen, the cellar, the workshop, and the field of townsfolk and farmers. For it is certain that God would have not only the church and the world order but also the house order established and upheld. All, therefore, who serve the latter purpose—father and mother first, then the children, and finally the servants and neighbors—are jointly serving God; for so He wills and commands.

In the light of this view of the matter a poor maid should have the joy in her heart of being able to say: Now I am cooking, making the bed, sweeping the house. Who has commanded me to do these things? My master and mistress have. Who has given them this authority over me? God has. Very well, then it must be true that I am serving not them alone but also God in heaven and that God must be pleased with my service.

THE ARENA THAT IS THE WORLD

AN UNGRATEFUL WORLD

The world is an aggregation of human beings who receive many paternal benefactions from God and then repay Him for them with blasphemies and ingratitude of every kind.

RUNNING TRUE TO FORM

The world is always true to itself, to wit, perfidious, the kingdom of Satan, and the enemy of Christ.

DECEIVING AND DECEIVED BY CHOICE

The world wants to deceive or be deceived. This is why the world has nothing to do with the truth.

IT'S HARD TO HELP THE WORLD

The world resembles a drunken peasant; when you lift him into the saddle on one side, he tumbles off on the other.

LONG ON PROMISE, SHORT ON PERFORMANCE

The world promises great things but delivers few. It acts like hosts who give their guests too little and console them with empty words.

THE WORLD DOESN'T GIVE ANYTHING FOR NOTHING

A man once rented an ass to ride on. The owner of the ass went on foot next to the rider. When it got too hot for the rider on the ass, he asked the owner to ride so that he might walk in the shade alongside. The owner of the ass was unwilling to do this because he had rented the ass to him for riding and not the ass's shadow. For the latter he would have to pay extra. This is a picture of the world, which doesn't give anything for nothing, not even a shadow.

DELIVERANCE THROUGH DEATH

EVEN THE SAINTS FEAR DEATH

I do not like to see people glad to die. I prefer to see them fear and tremble and turn pale before death but nevertheless pass through it. Great saints do not like to die. The fear of death is natural, for death is a penalty; therefore it is something sad. According to the spirit, one gladly dies; but according to the flesh, it is said: "Another will carry you where you do not wish to go." (John 21:18 RSV)

WHY DEATH IS BITTER FOR CHRISTIANS

Christians could easily bear death if they did not know it as evidence of the wrath of God. This knowledge makes death so bitter for us. But the heathen die in security. They do not see the wrath of God but imagine death to be the end of a man and say: It is merely a matter of one evil little hour. Cicero has pointedly said: After death we shall either be nothing at all, or we shall be altogether blessed. He practically says: Nothing evil can happen to us after death.

WHAT MAKES DEATH HARDER FOR ADULTS

A child of seven dies easiest, without fear of death. But as soon as we become adults, the awareness of death and hell begins, and we fear death.

SAFE IN THE GOOD SHEPHERD'S HANDS

He Himself will provide a place where my soul may continue to exist, He who was so concerned about it that He sacrificed His own life in order to redeem mine, this best of Shepherds and blessed Bishop of the souls of those who believed in Him! Nor am I the first on whom He begins to learn how to preserve the souls of His believers. Nor do I want my soul placed into my own hands and care, for in that case it would be devoured in a moment by the devil. But He has it in hand, and no one can tear it from Him. I am satisfied to know that there are many mansions in my Father's house.

THE LAST HOUR—A HEAVENLY GIFT

The hour of our death is a heavenly gift for which we should constantly ask God and daily prepare ourselves so that with Simeon and Paul we look forward to our departure and our gain with pious longing.

DEATH SEPARATING MARRIAGE PARTNERS

There is no sweeter union than that in a good marriage. Nor is there any death more bitter than that which separates a married couple. Only the death of children comes close to this; how much this hurts I have myself experienced.

CHRIST HAS DESTROYED DEATH

Astonishing is the stupidity of a man who fears death. Death is common to all men, and nobody can escape it. Cicero was able to comfort himself very well as a heathen in the first book of the Tusculans. How much more ought Christians do this, for they have Christ, the destroyer of death, and have [eternal] life and the resurrection. Even if we'd like to live longer, it's a brief interval at best.

SENSE OF RESIGNATION

I'm subject to the will of God. I've given myself up to Him altogether. He'll take care of everything. I'm sure that He won't die because He is Himself life and resurrection. Whoever lives and believes in Him shall not die; though he die, yet shall he live (John 11:25). Therefore I submit to His will.

AT HOME IN HEAVEN

WHAT WILL WE DO IN HEAVEN?

I often think about it, but I cannot understand what we shall do to pass away the time; for there will be no change there, no labor, food, drink, and transactions. But I hold that in God we shall have enough to keep us occupied. Therefore Philip says very well: "Lord, show us the Father, and we shall be satisfied" (John 14:8 RSV). God will be the most delightful Object to contemplate.

THE SECOND PARADISE IS BETTER

The future glory will be far greater than was the glory of Adam in Paradise before the Fall. Had Adam remained in innocence and not violated the command of God, he would have begotten children but would not have forever remained in this state in Paradise. On the contrary, he would have been received into yonder glory, not by death—for he would have remained immortal—but by translation.

WE KNOW LITTLE ABOUT HEAVEN

When I hung at my mother's breasts, I did not know much about the manner in which I would eat or drink or live later on. We understand far less what sort of life yonder one will turn out to be.

Human reason can't grasp it by speculation. With our thoughts we can't get beyond the visible and physical. No man's heart comprehends eternity. One might suppose that according to the saying, "Even pleasure becomes burdensome," one would get tired of eternity. What pleasure is like in eternity we can't imagine.

DEGREES OF GLORY

Although one saint may be more glorious than another in yonder life, the same eternal life will be enjoyed by all. Nonetheless there will be a difference such as that now existing here on earth, where one is stronger, more beautiful, and more eloquent than another and yet all enjoy the same physical existence. So there will also be many degrees of splendor and glory in yonder life, as St. Paul teaches 1 Cor. 15:40; and yet all will be alike in the enjoyment of the same eternal blessedness and delight, and there will be but *one* glory for all, because we shall all be the children of God.

WHERE ETERNAL LIFE BEGINS

Eternal life begins here, in our hearts; for when we begin to believe in Christ, after we have been baptized, then, according to faith and the Word, we are liberated from death, from sin, and from the devil. Therefore we have the beginning of life eternal and its first fruits in this life, a sort of mild foretaste; we have entered the lobby; but soon, divested of this flesh, we shall fully appreciate all.

We should learn to bring our eyes, our hearts, and souls to bear upon yonder life in heaven and in a lively hope await it with joy. For if we would be Christians, the ultimate objects of our quest should not be marrying, giving in marriage, buying, selling, planting, building—activities that Christ says (Matt. 24:37 ff.; Luke 17:26 ff.) the wicked will be engaged in especially before the Last Day. To be sure, we too must use these things in order to satisfy the needs of the body. But our ultimate quest should be something better and higher: the blessed inheritance in heaven that does not pass away.

MANY ENJOYMENTS

In the future life we'll have enjoyment of every kind and the whole earth will be adorned with many trees and all things that are pleasant to look at. If we have our Lord God we'll have enough. We'll be children of God. I don't believe that we shall all be of the same stature, and there will be no marriage; otherwise, everybody will want to be a woman or a man.

LUTHER: THE BEGINNING
AND THE END

WHAT LUTHER DISCOVERED

These words, "the just" and "righteousness," were lightning and thunder in my conscience under the papacy, and merely hearing them mentioned terrified me. In this tower [of The Black Cloister, Wittenberg, Germany], in which there was a special place for the monks, I once meditated on these words: The just lives by faith (Hab. 2:4), and, the righteousness of God (Rom. 1:17). Then it suddenly came to my mind: If we are to live righteously because of righteousness by faith and this righteousness of God is intended to save everyone who believes, it follows that righteousness is by faith and life by righteousness. And my conscience and spirit were lifted up, and I was made certain that it is the righteousness of God which justifies and saves us. And immediately these words became sweet and delightful words to me. That art the Holy Spirit taught me in this tower.

HOW LUTHER DEALT WITH THE DEVIL

Satan has often said to me: What if your teaching . . . were false? He has often caught me so unawares that I broke into a sweat. But finally I replied: Go and speak with God, who has commanded us to hear Christ (Matt. 17:5). This Christ must do everything. Therefore he who would be a Christian must let Christ answer for all.

HE TRUSTED IN CHRIST

Let us rely on Christ. Whether God decides to take me hence this hour or tomorrow, I intend to leave the reputation behind that I am resolved to recognize Christ as Lord. And I do this not only on the basis of Scripture but also on the basis of personal experience, for the name of Christ has often helped me when no one else could help. Thus I have on my side the substance and the words, experience and Scripture; and God has given me both in great measure. But temptations made me work hard for this trust; yet that was very good for me.

GROWING TIRED

I hold that there has been no one in a thousand years to whom the world has been more hostile than to me. I am hostile to her too and know nothing further in life which I desire. I am very tired of living. May our Lord God come very soon and take me away, and may He particularly come with His Judgment Day.

Compiled by N. Alfred Balmer